HOW TO SUCCESSFULLY DOMINATE LINKEDIN AND LINKEDIN MARKETING

ALUN HILL

CONTENTS

About the Author	v
Reviews Of Courses And Training By Alun Hill	vii
Acknowledgements	xvii
Disclaimer	xix
Introduction	xxi

1. What is LinkedIn All About?	1
2. What can LinkedIn do for your Business?	4
3. Shocking LinkedIn Marketing Facts to Consider	8
4. LinkedIn Walkthrough	13
5. Talent Solutions	19
6. Marketing Solutions	22
7. Sales Solutions	25
8. Learning Solutions	28
9. LinkedIn Company Pages	31
10. LinkedIn Groups	35
11. Advertise on LinkedIn	38
12. Smart Ways to Get Leads on LinkedIn	41
13. How to do Affiliate Marketing on LinkedIn	45
14. Using the LinkedIn Feed for Market Research	49
15. Small Business Resources to Help You Get More Out of LinkedIn	53
16. Going Premium with LinkedIn	56
17. Do's and Don'ts	59
18. Premium Tools and Services to Consider	64
19. Shocking Case Studies	69
20. Frequently Asked Questions	74

ABOUT THE AUTHOR

Alun Hill is the owner of 32 profitable online and offline business.

He credits much of this success to his study and mastering of LinkedIn.

He has been using LinkedIn for many years and is widely recognised as the "go-to" person for help and advice.

He has taught LinkedIn to individuals and groups worldwide, both in person and via online courses - there clients ranged from one person start ups to well known corporations.

Clients include those looking to improve their own business sales as well as many who realised that there was a massive, well paid, market for trained LinkedIn Consultants, both freelance and employed.

This book is now in the 4th edition and is fully updated for Fall 2017.

If you would like further training or help, his website at

AlunHill.com offers his free 70 page monthly magazine, showing many ways to improve your income and lifestyle.

The newsletter contains no adverts or affiliate links etc - just independent, usable, advice and help.

His many courses on setting up and running small businesses, asking "Would An Extra $1,000 A Month Help You?", are available at Tetmo.com.

These have already sold over 250,000 copies, worldwide.

Alun can be reached at alun@alunhill.com

REVIEWS OF COURSES AND TRAINING BY ALUN HILL

"Not only is the content great, but Alun's modeling of his methods is worth it's weight in gold. "

— Linda Schneider

"I find Alun Hill to be very "down to earth" despite his huge success(es). It's great to learn from someone who has done so well and you can tell he enjoys helping others. Great course. Thanks Alun! "

— Susan Gast

"I enjoy the insightful material that is at the same time factual with a touch of his English to keep it interesting. Well done."

— Rich Aanrich

"Alun has a great way of presenting. Speaks clear - has a bit of humor and last but not least VERY knowledgable. I learned more in his course than I did in 4 years of High School! "

— Kevin LaCombe

"I liked the course because it is very practical and business-oriented in its approach. It contains enough technical details where required. I believe this course will help me design a course well. Thank you Alun."

— Sundara Nagarajan

"I have taken my time to listen to the course several times. I find the course engaging and the instructor is unselfish in providing expert knowledge. Each lecture has been a tremendous help to me as a future instructor. I really appreciate the time and effort Alun has taken to perfect his courses. Thank you again for this excellent information!"

— Dr Shandra Terrell Williams

"Alun is a great teacher and his approach is very thorough. Tons of great information in his course. I'll follow it to the letter!"

— Perry Lawrence

"Thanks to Alun for giving his students everything they need to know to create their own course, and start teaching online. Highly recommended."

— Tommy Donbavand

"Alun gives a ton of information. It is very enlightening to see a pro in action."

— Alex Ticknovich

"This is the best course I ever took, and I am starting to see results. Alun Hill is Godsend for me. How can I ever thank him enough."

— Pranay Kumar

"All of them are in this course. Quality, clarity, packed with relevant information and best practices. You won't find better."

— Ryan Carter

"Alun is very knowledgeable and clear in his instructions, I really enjoyed the course and there was lots of information given."

— Bev Revill

"He (Alun Hill) is someone who is extraordinarily thorough with a great deal of empathy for the purchaser of his coursework. I really admire his dogged attention to detail. There are others who put things together too quickly to make a quick buck but with Alun you can be sure that this guy will do a super professional job before he signs his name off to something. Very impressive."

— Louis Geo

"Thank you for this course. I did learn many new strategies, working towards my first course. I think everyone should do this course to get best output."

— Narendra J. Mane

"I learned a great deal from the course. The instructor is very knowledgeable, the course quality was great and the material presented was well organized."

— Rhonda Jordan

"I enrolled in Alun's course because he said he would help me learn how to set up a business using Amazon's FBA program. That's exactly what he did! ... I have completed several of Mr. Hill's courses and all of them have delivered as promised."

— Timothy A. Storlie

"I finished the course and now I am a professional seller on Amazon.com ... Thank you so much for the great course and support."

— Suman Chandra Das

"This course was very informative! You definitely have to take initiative and use common sense in addition to following the instructions given. I've already received my test batch of products, have barcodes, and will be sending them to amazon soon. I didn't see the need to wait for a sale to say how great the course is, because it is straight forward and exposes you to various aspects of this business which you may neglect on a daily basis. Thanks Alun!"

— Vernon Solomon

"Alun provides great content with this extra income course. It is very thorough and he offers his professional knowledge, wit and style to this easy-to-follow course. A top rating for a top instructor!"

— Jim Peinkofer

"Alun is a good teacher, easy to understand and so many examples how someone can reach their goals with their Amazon business."

— Edward Bush

"I have just finished Alun Hill's course ... Excellent

course, I learnt a lot of stuff and I look forward to implementing it shortly. Alun clearly enjoys what he is doing which makes it so much more fun to learn. I look forward to doing more of Alun's courses. Thanks Alun! "

— Alan

"This course is a life changer for me. Alun Hill is open and expressive and extremely clear in his teachings. His advice is outstanding and his dedication to his students is impressive. Thank you for this course!"

— Joanne Reid

"I ... didn't realize how risk could be limited, and how it could be done almost anyplace in world. It's simpler than I would have thought possible. Thanks a lot for this course."

— Richard Stooker

"Alun, you're straight forward, frank, honest, and knowledgeable. Thank you for that."

— Michael Hulleman

"This course is extremely helpful and well presented; Alun Hill is an excellent instructor has provided a wealth of information from start to finish."

— Xosasun

"This course is a perfect one for those like me who has never (an) done online business before. I first came to the course with zero knowledge of what to do to... Alun has compiled lots of useful links and materials. You'd expect to read a lot in this course ... I learned all the basics; I love his videos the most. Those are exceptional and easily understandable. I rate this course a 5-star rating because: 1. I love his videos. 2. I love the way he is responsive to the discussion. 3. He has updated the courses. 4. The course is easy to follow. "

— Lengieng Ing

"A great instructor, tells it like it is. Great ideas and a good attitude toward issues. Thank you!"

— Christine Tripp

"Alun's course is very informative and helped me launch my first course. Thanks Alun. "

— Ben Kumanovski

"Great course, amazing insights and great building blocks moving forward. Alun Hill is obviously a well-gifted communicator and made everything sound super interesting."

— Marc Cichon

"Clearly a high quality guide! Real proof and you will need a notebook to write all this wisdom on paper!"

— Nicky Wong

"I loved the simplicity of Alun's message as well as the very high quality of his sound recordings and no fuss videos. I was able to make notes while he talked without having to keep watching him. The content is complete, the suggestions are easy to understand and I hope simple to implement on my end! Thanks Alun!"

— Tania M Adams

"This is one really good course. A lot of information's

inside ... I think this course is for anyone who is looking for new business or just to create some extra stream of income."

— Danilo Stojkovic

"What I liked best at the start was Alun's reassurance that there are no quick fixes or dodges. His advice is about doing the work, but learning from his mistakes and his successes in how to do it. Some excellent advice that I shall be following as I start work on marketing my first course. Thank you Alun."

— Dr Mike Clayton

"I've taken heaps of marketing courses and none has been as efficient as this one. Alun is very knowledgable and he is a great person to learn from. In just a week I was able to increase my revenues by applying what Alun explains in this course. I would never be able to thank him enough!"

— Pauline Hanuise

"Take Alun Hill's courses if you want to be successful and make money. Not only does he give lots of useful information, but he shows you in real time how he does it with his own statistics and accounts. I've taken three of his courses now and I am working on the fourth. My own (business) has increased by a huge percentage in just the last two weeks following my implementing Alun's suggestions and secret information. I highly recommend you take this course and any of Alun's other courses."

— Teresa L Greenway

"i'm giving Alun five stars because this course changed the way I think, thank you Alun."

— Mohammed

"This course is excellent, a great introduction to FBA. Alun provides an enormous amount of information which is very helpful. The course quality is very good. Thank you Alun!"

— Anthea P

"Alun's course was hugely helpful in increasing my own success! ... When Alun showed clearly ... exactly how he went about setting his courses up for success here in this course, I was motivated to do better in my own courses. Within a month of enrolling in this course, I saw a 10x increase in my sales after applying some of the small changes Alun recommended AND increasing the amount of time and effort I put into my courses. I now work on my courses first thing every day and have to say Alun Hill has been one of the single most helpful instructors to me for inspiring my success and the success of others!"

— Jerry Banfield

"I just want to thank you for such a rich and intensive course ... what you did is you saved me several months of searching and experimentation etc ... To sum up - thank you a lot."

— Aleksey Grebeshkov

"... I used this course to promote my small business

products and services! It works! Best money I've spent in a long time! "

— Curtis Arnold

Copyright © 2017 by Alun Hill

All rights reserved.

No part of this book may be reproduced in any form or by any electronic or mechanical means, including information storage and retrieval systems, without written permission from the author, except for the use of brief quotations in a book review.

ACKNOWLEDGEMENTS

Alun would like to thank the various teams at LinkedIn for all their help in making the previous 3 editions such a success.

He wishes it known, of course, that this book is his own work and that he is not affiliated in any way with LinkedIn, nor have they had any input on the final publication.

DISCLAIMER

This work may not be copied, sold, used as content in any manner or your name put on it until you buy sufficient rights to sell it or distribute it as your own from us and the authorized reseller/distributer.

Every effort has been made to be accurate in this publication. The publisher does not assume any responsibility for errors, omissions or contrary interpretation. We do our best to provide the best information on the subject, but just reading it does not guarantee success. You will need to apply every step of the process in order to get the results you are looking for.

This publication is not intended for use as a source of any legal, medical or accounting advice. The information contained in this guide may be subject to laws in the United States and other jurisdictions. We suggest carefully reading the necessary terms of the services/products used before applying it to any activity which is, or may be, regulated. We do not assume any responsibility for what you choose to do with this information. Use your own judgment.

Any perceived slight of specific people or organizations, and any resemblance to characters living, dead or otherwise, real or fictitious, is purely unintentional.

Some examples of past results are used in this publication; they are intended to be for example purposes only and do not guarantee you will get the same results. Your results may differ from ours. Your results from the use of this information will depend on you, your skills and effort, and other different unpredictable factors.

It is important for you to clearly understand that all marketing activities carry the possibility of loss of investment for testing purposes. Use this information wisely and at your own risk.

INTRODUCTION

Welcome to the latest (4th) edition - designed to take you by the hand and walk you through the process of getting the most out of LinkedIn.

I'm very excited to have you here, and I know that this will be very helpful for you.

This exclusive training will show you step-by-step, topic by topic, and tool by tool, what you need to know to **"Dominate LinkedIn and LinkedIn Marketing"**, in the easiest way possible, using the most effective tools and in the shortest time ever.

This training is comprised of 20 chapters organized into 4 sections.

Here is exactly what you are going to learn:

Section 1: LinkedIn Basics

In Chapters 1 through 4, we'll talk about:

INTRODUCTION

- What is LinkedIn all about?
- What LinkedIn can do for your Business?
- Shocking LinkedIn Marketing Facts to Consider
- LinkedIn Walkthrough

Section 2: Linkedin Business Solutions

In Chapters 5 through 8, we'll talk about:

- Talent Solutions
- Marketing Solutions
- Sales Solutions
- Learning Solutions

Section 3: Marketing on LinkedIn – Step by Step

In Chapters 9 through 16, we'll talk about:

- LinkedIn Company Pages
- LinkedIn Groups
- Advertise on LinkedIn
- Smart Ways to Get Leads on LinkedIn
- How to do Affiliate Marketing on LinkedIn
- Using the LinkedIn Feed for Market Research
- Small business resources to help you get more out of LinkedIn
- Going Premium with LinkedIn

Section 4: Additional Tips to consider

INTRODUCTION

In Chapters 17 through 20, we'll talk about:

- Do's and Don'ts
- Premium tools and Services to consider
- Shocking Case Studies
- Frequently Asked Questions

WHAT IS LINKEDIN ALL ABOUT?

Social media platforms took the internet by storm more than a decade ago and they have been one of the biggest sources of online activity ever since.

They were all about minimal user interaction and only used by very specific demographics.

But then Facebook entered the picture and it changed the way that things were made online forever, mainly because from then on every place on the internet has made the effort to offer some kind of social feature to their visitors.

It also gave birth to the phenomenon of social networks, and now there is a social network for basically anything.

The later focalized approach to designing social networks targeting a specific activity and a specific demographic is what made possible the conception of LinkedInm - famous for being a social network mainly used by job seekers and head hunters.

But describing LinkedIn as such barely does it justice.

LinkedIn can be best described as a social network with features designed to benefit the business community as a whole.

The main goal of this social network is to connect its members on a professional level.

Just like any other social networking site, LinkedIn allows people to join it for free and to create a social profile.

Whereas other social networks are mostly designed as billboards for people's interests, hobbies, everyday moments and thoughts, LinkedIn is designed to highlight career related information.

LinkedIn profiles emphasize information such as professional or labor skills, employment history and education.

Also, unlike common social networking sites, social contacts are not called followers or friends, but "connections", as to establish a professional tone to interactions made by people on the platform.

These connections allow members to connect with people with whom they have worked, gone to school with, or with people that they know on a professional level, whether online or offline.

The big advantage that LinkedIn offers to its regular users is that it allows them to be discovered by companies looking for employees thanks to the massive amount of data that LinkedIn users provide the platform with, including job titles, geographical locations, skillsets, industry information and much more.

On a purely practical level, this means that users looking for new career options as well as for ways to expand their professional reach can use LinkedIn as a great platform to boost their efforts because it is a powerful way to connect with employers as well as with other people that might help them to learn a lot more about their own career path.

And much like on Facebook, users can customize their LinkedIn accounts so they are served only the best career related info, including personalized job listings.

Also, a LinkedIn profile is currently valued like a well-crafted resume, and lots of people have had success in using the platform to find their dream jobs!

LinkedIn can also be used as a great educational resource, as lots of famous business people have LinkedIn profiles that any user can follow to find helpful tips from the most seasoned of professionals from around the world.

So now you know that LinkedIn is a great platform to kick start a professional career and to find the perfect job without ever leaving your house, but what if you are already running your own company?

How can LinkedIn help you grow your business?

WHAT CAN LINKEDIN DO FOR YOUR BUSINESS?

*O*k, so it is obvious by now that LinkedIn represents a major shift in what the social media revolution offered to the public because it showed people that it was completely possible to create a social marketing platform that could be as user friendly as it was serious.

Not only because it got away with the "trivial" nature of every other social media platform and allowed people to use their social profiles as online resumes for free, because it also allowed companies to establish an online presence that didn't have anything to do with entertaining their social audience.

And you can thank this to the fact that, perhaps inadvertently, LinkedIn slowly became a sort of data rich environment, a place containing the type of information about the modern job market that companies would have paid millions to just peek at.

And that is perhaps why, in 2016, Microsoft paid almost $27 billion for it. What does it say about its potential to drive business then? Let us provide you a few reasons why we think that your business will benefit from being on LinkedIn.

You can use LinkedIn to hire the best talent on the net

LinkedIn is a great place for job seekers to find their dream job precisely because it is also a great place for businesses and companies of all sizes to attract the best talent and to recruit the best employees from the world's largest talent pool.

Businesses can access recruiting tools that will allow them to post jobs to target the right candidates for the job offered, to find and source active as well as passive talent and to seize the collection of skills offered by these talents to further build their brands.

You can use LinkedIn as a marketing platform

And best of all, as a marketing platform to reach the largest professional audience in the world. You can easily reach the best fit for your business so you can further develop your brand, increase your visibility and make new business connections possible.

Marketing options on LinkedIn are pretty varied, and they include powerful promotional tools such as sponsored content that can reach people on any device, dynamic ads to market to professionals on the go, and display ads for those doing their job at the office, among others.

You can use LinkedIn to Sell

LinkedIn can increase your commercial potential by providing you with a platform that is designed to drive social selling efforts with real time sales intelligence. And what this means is that LinkedIn is backing an entire platform with non-intrusive sales solutions.

You can use LinkedIn as a learning platform

LinkedIn is a professionally oriented platform, which makes education its second nature. As such, you can use LinkedIn to keep your team's skillset up to date with current educational and developmental trends.

The workplace learning tools offered by LinkedIn will help your team to develop two of the most valued skills in the current and future industries: people management and soft skills, which include creativity and communication.

LinkedIn learning tools will also help your company to close the gap between soft and technical skills, which will help your company to become a business of the future! With over 10,000 online training and development courses available, LinkedIn is the perfect platform for ongoing professional development.

What else can your business benefit from by being on LinkedIn?

- You can create shareable content that can help you connect with a wide professional audience. You can create content with the potential to add value to people's professional lives, which can easily create engagement and foster a following for your company on the platform.

- LinkedIn offers you multiple ways to feed information to its members by allowing you to post content using slide shares for business presentations, blog posts, infographics, webinars, podcasts and videos. You will just have to choose which ones are the best fits for your audience.
- LinkedIn will not hinder your efforts to provide your audience with relevant content, and you will be able to post as many times as your content allows you to. In fact, LinkedIn encourages businesses to release quality content as much as possible!
- You can use your company profile to drive more sales for products and services that your company develops. You will just have to tell your potential customers about their benefits!
- You can use your business profile to differentiate yourself from your competition. Sharing news and information about your company culture on a regular basis can easily help you to establish a company persona.
- Your employees can use their LinkedIn profiles to enhance your company's visibility, as engaged and satisfied employees are a great way to communicate healthy social proof!

SHOCKING LINKEDIN MARKETING FACTS TO CONSIDER

We live in a world that is becoming more and more interconnected with each passing day. New technologies and ways to implement it are now the norm, and they're changing people's lives in a way that was simply unthinkable of in previous years.

One of those technologies is social media, which allowed people from all around the globe to connect on a very personal basis regardless of distance, and the best part is that the implementation of social media in everyday life is pretty much multidimensional.

And you can thank this to the fact that social media was not monopolized by neither of the social networking companies in the market because each one of them plays on a different field, and each one offers its users a different set of features.

But the good news for marketers and company owners

like you and us is that each platform is designed to drive business quite efficiently, which is more practical when you consider that LinkedIn is a business oriented platform. Here are some LinkedIn marketing facts to start your day!

- A whopping 70% of LinkedIn users are from outside the US. You wouldn't think that this number could be relevant until you consider that such a large number of demographics from outside the United States can allow you reach a global minded, international audience that can help you to understand overseas markets.
- 41% of millionaires from around the world use LinkedIn, which means that the next investor to inject some financial aid to your business can be just around the corner!
- 79% of business to business marketers consider that social media, especially LinkedIn, is an effective marketing channel for any type of business.
- In fact, nowadays 80% of business to business leads are generated on LinkedIn
- 43% of marketers have said that they have sourced customers from LinkedIn, which is a really big number when you take into account that LinkedIn is mostly geared towards employers and job seekers.
- A cool 49% of the traffic going to company

websites comes from LinkedIn, which is a significant portion considering how many social networks are sharing the market with LinkedIn. This also means that 49% of traffic going to company websites is already qualified for doing business!

- 94% of business to business marketers use LinkedIn to distribute content, and on average, 10 pieces of that content are consumed by users before they make a purchasing decision, which means that your content has to be relevant enough as to break the 10 piece mark!
- 39% of LinkedIn users pay for a premium subscription, which means that almost 40% of users are willing to pay for exclusive content and connections.
- Men are statistically more likely to use LinkedIn than women, with 32% of LinkedIn members being men against 21% of female members, which means that you should be wise when designing your marketing campaigns
- This fact should come as a no brainer, but it bears relevance nonetheless, and it is worthy of being shared: While social networks such as Facebook and twitter are mostly used to share topics like sports and celebrity news, LinkedIn is strictly used to share two specific types of news: business and professional news.

What does this mean for your business? That while you can easily attract traffic by sharing entertaining news on other social networks, there is simply no point in sharing similar news on LinkedIn. Instead, your marketing has to focus on content that is relevant to industries and business activities.

- Only 23% of LinkedIn members use the site on a daily basis, with over 50% of members using it on a weekly basis, sometimes less. This might be because of the professionally focused, busy nature of most LinkedIn users, but regardless of the cause you have to plan your LinkedIn marketing around non-daily reactions.
- LinkedIn is the largest professional database on the planet, with way more business information than any other site on the planet! That is because LinkedIn is home to over 3 million company pages and 300 million professional profiles.

The best part is that you will only need to use the search function to make use of this information, which can save your business a small fortune on data analysis and research.

- There are over 200 conversations per minute occurring on LinkedIn groups at any given time, which means that whatever your business goal is, you have to leverage this reach through your business presence.

LINKEDIN WALKTHROUGH

Ok, so you are now realizing that LinkedIn is an amazingly designed social media platform that is perfect for professionals, business owners and decision makers across any industry, and you're convinced about the benefits of getting yourself a LinkedIn profile.

And as with any other social networking site that you join, you'll have to go beyond your profile if you really want to learn anything that you can use it for. In this video we are going to show you everything that you will find on LinkedIn while signed into your account.

The first thing that you will be greeted with when you log into your LinkedIn account is your LinkedIn feed, which also serves as the "home" section of your LinkedIn account, as clicking on the "home" button on the dashboard menu from any other section will take you here.

This section along with your profile are the ones that

resemble other social media sites, as you will be able to post content and updates in the "share an article, photo or update" field. There you will see the "write an article" and the "image" buttons. The former will allow you to create written content, and the latter will allow you to upload an image. You can use the "post" button to upload your content.

On your left you will find a box that links to your profile, and on the right will be featured ads. Now, when you scroll down a bit you will find what is actually served on the feed, so let's take a quick look at it.

First you will find the "people you may know" box, which will show you LinkedIn profiles that you can add based on your own profile. Scroll down further and you will find the "suggested for you" box, which is where you will find content posted by other professionals on the platform and by companies.

Below the advertising box you will find a quick access menu with links to other LinkedIn sections, including the "business services" app, which you can access from your account dashboard menu as well. Let's now check this dashboard menu, which is located on top.

From left to right, you will find a quick link button to LinkedIn's home page and a search bar, and we will go into detail on how to use this bar alongside the LinkedIn feed for research in a later video.

Next up you have the "home" tab, which will take you to the home section when you click on it. The "network" tab will show you a section where you can manage your professional network. On the left side you will see a box from where you can see your current connections, and from which you can use the "find connections" link to locate other professional profiles on the platform.

You can see your "pending invitations" and act upon them by accepting or rejecting them, and you can use your email address to locate LinkedIn profiles attached to email addresses from your contact list. Lastly, you will have a list of "people you may know" with profile suggestions.

Let's now look at the "jobs" section. Here you will be able to manage your job postings and applications. There you will be able to manage your "saved jobs", your "applied jobs" and to "post a job" if you want to hire talent for your company.

In the "jobs that you might be interested in" box you will find job posts as job suggestions based on the information on your profile. Now, you can also search for jobs in this section by using the two search bars on top.

The first one will allow you to "search jobs by title, keyword or company", and the second will allow you to use "city, state, postal code or country" as your keywords to find job postings. You can use both search bars to find job postings using keywords as filters and then clicking on the "search" button.

Let's now go over the "messaging" tab. In this section you will be able to manage your correspondence with other members and companies. At first glance you will be able to access your received messages, which will be featured on the left, just like if it were an email inbox.

Over this message list you will have a search bar to locate specific messages, and you can use the "compose a new message" button to create correspondence. In the "notifications" tab you will be able to access and manage your notifications. Let's now look at the "me" tab.

The "me" tab works as a drop down menu that will allow you to access your profile, your account settings and to manage your activity. The first option available is the "view my profile" link, which will take you to your LinkedIn profile. Now, it will not only allow you to view your profile, but to also edit it from top to bottom.

Here you will find the option to "add new profile section" to include sections with professional information such as "background" information including "work experience", "education", "volunteer experience", your "skills" and your "accomplishments".

You can use the "edit public profile" feature to customize how people that are not signed up on LinkedIn view your profile, and you can use the "add profile in another language" feature to create your profile in a different language to make it easier for professionals and businesses from other locations to check your information.

Then you will have the options to update your background photo, to edit your intro information including profile picture, names, headline and current job position. You can also edit your "contact and personal info", to add education and work experience levels.

Back on the "me" menu you will have the "account" and

the "manage" sub menus. Let's look at the first option from the "account" sub menu by clicking on the "settings and privacy" tab. There you will be able to edit your "account" settings including your basic user information such as email address, password and language, your "partners and third party" settings, your "subscriptions" settings and other advanced "account settings".

From there you will also be able to edit your "privacy" settings and your "communications" settings. Now, in the "help center" tab from this sub menu you will be able to access the entire support library. The "language" tab can be used to easily change your language.

Let's now look at the "manage" sub menu starting on the "posts and activity" tab. From this section you will be able to check and manage your activity on the platform, which includes your shared links, your posts and your articles. The "job postings" tab will allow you to manage your job postings from a single section, as long as you are signed up to use the "LinkedIn Recruiter" solution.

The "sign out" tab will allow you to sign out of LinkedIn with a simple click. Let's close this walkthrough by checking out the last tab on your dashboard, the "work" tab. In this tab you will find a menu with business oriented solutions.

These solutions are offered in the form of different LinkedIn products, including learning products, job postings, advertising products, LinkedIn groups, and the SlideShare platform, among others. You will also be able to access LinkedIn business services from this tab including "talent solutions", "sales solutions" and "learning solutions".

Lastly, you will be able to use the "create a company page" tab to go to the company page set up section to create your own business profile the easy way. We are going to delve deeper into each one of these features in our following videos, so make sure to stay tuned and don't miss a thing!

TALENT SOLUTIONS

LinkedIn is, as you might have seen by now, a platform that takes great pride in the way that it allows companies and businesses of all sizes to get in touch with the type of talent that represents the greatest fit for proper organizational development.

So, one of the greatest reasons why your business will greatly benefit from having a presence on the largest professional networking platform is because it can provide you with the best variety of recruiting tools that will allow you to meet your next hire.

LinkedIn talent solutions offer talent seekers three types of solutions. You can start with job postings that target the right type of candidate for any job and then to find qualified applicants that can accelerate your hiring efforts.

You can post jobs by simply signing up to use LinkedIn as an employer, and you can hire up to two hires a year with a free account, but if you plan to hire more than three hires a year you can contact LinkedIn to request the feature that will allow you to swap more than three job slots at a time!

LinkedIn also allows you to source active and passive talent from the platform through sourcing tools that will enable you to quickly hire quality candidates, which is possible when you use the "recruiter lite" and the "recruiter" tools.

The "recruiter lite" tool is a lightweight solution for companies looking for a few hires a year, and you can get started for free, but if your goal is to tap into the largest pool of talent and access LinkedIn's massive network of professionals for hire your obvious choice would be to use the full "recruiter" suite.

Another way to find talent to work for your organization is not by posting jobs or by navigating the database of professional profiles available on LinkedIn but by promoting your brand as an organization where top talent would likely want to collaborate with, and LinkedIn offers you the right type of tools to help you further build your brand and showcase your unique organizational culture.

Having a strong brand that stands out in this competitive job market is essential when it comes to attracting the right people through your doors, and LinkedIn has two solutions that will help you out on capitalizing the branding factor for your business.

First you have the "career pages" that can help you to showcase jobs that are tailored towards specific talent as well as to showcase your excellent work culture. Not to be confused with company pages, these career pages are designed to make your job postings to better stand out to potential candidates through awesomely targeted job opportunities.

And unlike company pages, where only information and content about your company is promoted, career pages are all about sharing your unique company story, attracting the best talent and also about measuring the impact of your employer brand on your recruiting goals.

Another highly targeted solution is the "work with us ads" solution, which are ads designed to capitalize on the high traffic ad space on your potential employee's profiles. These job ads on average get 50 times more engagement than typical recruitment ads and they drive interest to your job posts, to your career pages on all your other LinkedIn placements so you can stay ahead of your competition.

Talent solutions are available to enterprise companies to help them hire lots of people more efficiently, to small and medium sized businesses so they can easily add more candidates to their pipeline in order to grow their business, to search and staffing agencies so they can get more leads.

Nonprofits can also benefit from using LinkedIn talent solutions and get steep discounts to get more people working on their fundraising efforts. So now you know, next time you are looking for the perfect employee look no further!

MARKETING SOLUTIONS

*L*inkedIn is a great platform when it comes to nurturing a very important marketing factor known as outreach. Outreach, is the marketing practice of looking for individuals and organizations that can be interested in what a marketer or business has to offer, be it a product, a service or a business idea.

Doing marketing outreach on social media has become commonplace because social networking platforms make it easier for people and companies to reach people where they are most likely to hang out the most, and social media offers marketers the benefit of narrowing lead qualifying criteria thanks to targeted placements such as groups and company pages.

And because you are using LinkedIn for outreach, it might be a little easier to find the right prospects and clients simply because you already know what people are looking for. Yet this organic approach to outreach has its own inherent limitations, and LinkedIn offers you the right type of marketing solutions that will help you to avoid being hindered by limitations.

And what we mean by this is that LinkedIn gives you access to the right tools that will help you to easily direct your marketing to who matters the most so you can reach your ideal customers right on the largest professional network in the world.

These marketing solutions will allow you to build your brand, to raise awareness about it and to generate leads the right way on LinkedIn, with several marketing options available at your disposal that include paid advertising and company pages that can help you to take your marketing efforts to a whole new level.

Sponsored content for example can help you to boost your content and show the very best version of it to the world's largest professional audience on any device. Sponsored content solutions will allow you to use comprehensive targeting options to reach the exact type of audience that your business needs through native advertising, which will in turn help you to build meaningful relationships with your prospects.

Another direct marketing solution offered by LinkedIn includes "InMail" advertising, which is all about reaching the people that are most likely to support your business with valuable content, right in their LinkedIn email inboxes. Using InMail solutions will help you to easily send personalized messages to your prospects. This type of correspondence has helped many businesses to drive conversions by reaching others right where they are the most engaged.

Other solutions include dynamic social ads that will allow you to drive relevant responses with ads that correspond to the activity and profiles of the members of your target audience, sending highly personalized copy and dynamically generated advert imagery to LinkedIn members.

Advertising offered by LinkedIn marketing solutions also includes display ads that will help you to reach your target audience through accurate professional targeting technology. These display ads are highly visible and are specifically placed on high traffic areas on the LinkedIn platform only, and they operate on a fraud monitored environment to ensure maximum brand safety.

Lastly, text ads are also supported by the LinkedIn marketing solutions platform, which gives members eager to try out advertising options, a way to stay within a tight budget and at the same time attract new customers to their business using LinkedIn's fail safe pay per click advertising platform.

They are designed to drive traffic and generate quality leads, and you can pay for them on either a click or impression basis. Start leveraging the power of LinkedIn's marketing solutions today!

SALES SOLUTIONS

LinkedIn is a place where anything that is business related comes and goes, and sales are no different.

Because, in the end, what really matters is to use LinkedIn as a platform to close: to close connections, to close deals, to close a hiring interview, or to close sales.

That is why LinkedIn has made a great, significant effort into creating a sales solution for its more business oriented users, one which will allow them to get started in the world of social selling through a series of powerful ways to engage with potential buyers on the platform.

But before looking at the product offered as LinkedIn's sales solution, the following questions are worth answering: what is social selling and why is it important to integrate into your marketing plan?

Social selling is the act of using social media to drive sales by interacting directly with prospects on their preferred communication channel, which in our case is LinkedIn. And social marketing is important because it allows salespeople to drive 45% more business opportunities, it makes them 51% more likely to reach their sales quota and it also makes them 78% more successful than sellers that do not use social media.

So what is LinkedIn's sales solution then? Allow us to introduce you to LinkedIn's "sales navigator", a tool which will enable you to connect with LinkedIn based buyers and sellers in a whole new way.

Finding the right people whom to offer your products or services to can be a hit or miss situation in most cases, but the LinkedIn sales navigator will allow you to target the right buyers and companies thanks to a sophisticated algorithm that will give you lead recommendations that are tailor made for your needs.

The sales navigator tool will also give you the ability to understand what your buyers value the most through sales insights that aim to leverage more effective selling strategies. In this respect the sales navigator has the best tools to help you stay informed about your contacts and accounts, as that is the only way to transform cold calling into a warm, relevant conversation.

Because LinkedIn understands that creating successful sales campaigns is all about building great relationships with your clients, the sales navigator will also allow you to engage existing and potential customers with a personalized outreach approach.

This is easy to achieve because the sales navigator enables you to establish trust even before starting your initial conversation. In short, it is designed to understand your buyers' intent and follow up on it effectively.

The sales navigator comes in three flavors, and finding the one that is right for you depends on the size of your business operation and the number of features that you would need to run them properly.

These three Sales Navigator plans are the "Professional", "Team" and "Enterprise" suites. Features included on each plan include from 20 to 50 promoted emails per month, extended LinkedIn network access, advanced sales-specific search tools, automated lead and account recommendations, access to a sales focused learning center and a dedicated mobile app.

Features that are only available to "Professional" and "Enterprise" Sales Navigator users include customer relationship management widgets and synchronization, out of network unlocks, usage reporting, volume based and multi-year discounts, invoicing and a dedicated client relationship manager.

You can start using the "Professional" Sales Navigator suite with a free trial so you can get a test drive of what you will be able to achieve with it, and you will need to request a demo once you are ready to advance in your social selling efforts. So get ready to take your sales force to the next level!

LEARNING SOLUTIONS

Becoming a professional takes years of education, but a university title alone won't be enough once you enter the workforce because what makes a dedicated professional is real world expertise acquired from ongoing, continuous learning.

That is why LinkedIn has devised a series of Learning Solutions that can be accessed through its platform and through third party efforts that have transformed the world of online education over the past decades.

The benefits obtained by businesses using LinkedIn's on demand learning solutions include soft and people management skills training that will allow them to develop managers and leaders among their talent, the merging of soft and technical skills on a practical level and a boost of employee productivity of up to 50%!

These learning solutions are available for businesses that

want to develop improved leadership positions on their teams, including the development of managers and leaders at all levels, to adapt to the job market of the future by upskilling their entire workforce through education, to keep their employees more productive by teaching them to be comfortable around digital tools and to accelerate career development among their employees.

Higher education facilities such as colleges and universities can also benefit from allowing their faculties, staff and students to access LinkedIn learning solutions that will allow them to discover more inspiring content, to assign video tutorials and tools training for homework and to leave classroom time for concept mastery, to keep the staff skillset up to date and to further prepare students to join the workforce once they are out there!

LinkedIn also offers Learning Solutions to government agencies so they can better manage workforce development by maximizing their budgets through on demand e-learning. LinkedIn Learning solutions will allow government agencies to do more with less, to attract and retain employees, to close job related skill gaps and to promote self-paced learning.

This is possible because LinkedIn Learning solutions can help government agencies to maximize their training budgets thanks to its cost-effective approach at covering thousands of relevant educational topics, to prioritize learning opportunities as another employee benefit offered by the organization while also helping these employees to acquire soft and hard skills that they will need to be more productive in their roles.

Lastly, LinkedIn Learning Solutions are also available to libraries, and they can provide skill building job training opportunities and resources to library staff and patrons. Learning solutions offered by LinkedIn to libraries will allow them to provide their staff with the business and technical training that it needs in order to succeed.

These learning solutions also benefit the community that the libraries are located in because they can jump start advanced job search and digital literacy initiatives supported by the public.

The expert led learning provided with these solutions include studio quality videos and resources curated by industry experts and by working professionals, which can greatly help library staff to acquire the type of skills that they need to be more productive in their specific careers.

Providing all these institutions with amazing educational opportunities through LinkedIn is made possible by the Lynda.com sponsored learning solution, which combines 20 years of experience that back Lynda.com's expertise in developing high quality content with the LinkedIn platform, making it easier to identify and personalize the learning experience offered to each person involved in the learning process.

LINKEDIN COMPANY PAGES

*L*inkedIn might be a pretty different social networking site targeted at a pretty specific audience and with a very specific set of features as well, but at its very core it's still a social networking site nonetheless. This means that it still shares some social features with the rest of social networking sites.

But because this is LinkedIn we are talking about, we can expect to see a significant spin on how these features are presented and on the way that they serve the platform's members. Such is the case with the feature called "company pages" which is LinkedIn's version of social media fan pages.

Company pages are designed beyond the scope of simply sharing what you like with others and as such they work specifically to help you grow your company's presence on LinkedIn and in turn on the internet landscape overall. The good news is that getting started with company pages on LinkedIn is an easy, straightforward process packed with a lot of benefits for your business.

It all starts with you creating a free company page on LinkedIn, and the only requirements is that you have a LinkedIn account and a valid email address so LinkedIn can verify that you are apt to create a company page for your business.

Secondly, you'll have to customize your company profile to give it its proper professional look and feel. LinkedIn recommends you to start by giving your company page a cover image and a logo to bring it to life. The logo that you use on your company page will appear on search results when people search for your company, and will also appear on the profile of your employees for an improved corporate presence.

Once your company page is ready you will be ready to start attracting followers by adding links to promote your LinkedIn company page by linking it through your emails, blogs, websites, and through any other source and placement that you use to bring online traffic to your business.

One of the ways offered by LinkedIn for you to link to your company page is in the form of "company page follow buttons", which you can also use the same way that you would use your company page links, and you can easily install them on your preferred placements with the help of an easily to implement plugin!

Company pages are also a great way to increase your

potentially viral reach. This is because you can encourage your employees as well as your business leadership colleagues to add your company page to their profiles, which will help you to get more likes, comments and shares to expand your reach and the number of people in your audience.

Company pages will also help you to post and share content, and everybody knows that posting daily company updates is one of the most effective ways to attract engaged followers. News, articles, and even think pieces can help you to stir up conversation with your followers because each one of your company page updates will appear across your company network, including placements such as in the news feed and home pages of your company page followers.

You can promote your company pages through sponsored content updates that will help you to widen your reach beyond your network. Also, your company page can be used to attract and build your employer brand when you upgrade it to a career page

Creating company pages is easy enough, as you would only need to go to the "work" tab on your LinkedIn account's dashboard and then click on the "create a company page" button at the bottom of the menu. Then enter the name of your company in the "company name" field and a custom yet simple name to add at the end of your public LinkedIn URL that people can use to identify your company page on search results.

Check the verification box below to confirm that you are

the rightful owner or individual appointed to manage your company page and then click on "create page". Once you are done with this you will be ready to start customizing your company page on LinkedIn!

LINKEDIN GROUPS

One of the most recognizable things about any social media platform is groups. Groups are the way that social media users employ to share their common interest in a more direct way because it allows them to post any type of content for other like minded individuals in a single place.

Groups on LinkedIn are no different, and they are all about allowing like minded professionals to share the highlights of their trades, and these groups are of special interest to LinkedIn members because they are places where all kinds of career and business related information is shared in a more personal way.

LinkedIn members can access groups and group oriented features by going to the "work" tab on the LinkedIn account dashboard and clicking on the "groups" button. There they will find their group's feed, which is aptly called the group's highlights section.

Highlights from groups in this section are only shown when a member has joined groups in LinkedIn, and to find groups of interest a LinkedIn member simply has to click on the "discover groups" button featured in this section.

Here they will find groups recommendations based on their profile and professional data. When they find a group that they might be interested in they simply have to click on "ask to join" to send a request to join the group to the group administrators.

They can also stop a group from showing up on the discover groups feed by clicking on the "not interested" button featured beside the "ask to join" button on each group. Let's now look at the "my groups" tab from the group highlights section.

In this tab LinkedIn members can see which groups they have created and to manage them accordingly. It is also from this tab where LinkedIn members will be able to create groups of their own by simply clicking on the "create group" button.

The group creation process is pretty simple and straightforward. Users simply have to enter a group title, select and upload a group logo, to add a description for the group, to add rules if desired and to select whether their new group is "standard" or "unlisted".

"Standard" groups are groups that can be joined by about any LinkedIn member as long as their invited or their requests to join are approved, and members of these groups can freely invite other members.

"Unlisted" groups on the other hand are groups where only owners, managers and moderators from those groups can invite members to join. Also, unlisted groups do not appear on search results or in the "discover groups" feed.

Once members have set up their groups they simply have to click on " save changes" to have them go live on the platform. After creating a group, LinkedIn members will be able to manage group members, invitations, group content, templates and group details.

LinkedIn members can then go back to the "my groups" tab and use the settings icon to manage them individually. Alternatively, members can find groups using any keyword by going to LinkedIn's homepage and using the search bar.

Once the results are loaded members can click the "groups" tab on the search results to filter out groups found using the keyword entered as filter. And this is how you find, join and create groups on LinkedIn!

ADVERTISE ON LINKEDIN

One of the things that makes LinkedIn an awesomely unique social media platform is its targeted approach at making itself useful for a very specific audience, this audience being made up of professionals and business managers from all locations and demographics.

This is especially good news for marketers, and while it might be true that organic reach on LinkedIn is amazing as it already is, there is also a very large degree of truth to the fact that paid advertising can play a huge part on widening your reach on the platform.

The good news is that LinkedIn offers its own native advertising solutions. That said, by advertising on LinkedIn, you will be able to reach your ideal customers on the largest professional network on the planet.

This is because advertising on LinkedIn works in a unique way that can help businesses of all sizes to achieve their goals. For starters, advertising on LinkedIn gives marketers access to what is perhaps the most targeted audience of any place on the internet, with over 500 million active professionals using the platform, and you can target them by attributes such as job title and industry among many others.

LinkedIn's advertising network is very practical at allowing you to create easy and effective ads, and whether your goal is to generate leads, create brand awareness or drive sales, LinkedIn ads can help you.

The LinkedIn advertising network is also efficient at helping you to control your budget and costs because it allows you really flexible pricing options, allowing you to get started on any budget and to stop your ads at any time.

You can easily create LinkedIn ads in a few minutes, and you have a nice variety of ad types to reach your prospects wherever they are and wherever they go without being intrusive.

Sponsored content ads, for example, can help you to boost your content across all devices so you can promote your company updates to a very targeted audience on desktop, mobile phones and tablets with a responsive design on the most viewed professional news feed.

Sponsored "InMail" ads on the other hand will allow you to deliver personalized adverts directly to people's LinkedIn inboxes, which has been found to drive more conversions than email marketing!

Text ads are a simpler advertising solution for LinkedIn

members because it allows them to start generating leads in mere minutes as creating a text ad only requires adding a compelling headline, a description and a small 50 by 50 image. This easy setup is what will allow you to get to your leads faster than you could imagine.

LinkedIn ads have been designed with any budget and goal in mind. For instance, the LinkedIn ad network will allow you to bid for your targeted audience on an auction basis, which means that you can bid against other advertisers to reach your target audience.

The good news is that you can choose your own "cost per click" or "cost per thousand impressions" to only compete with advertisers on an even budget, and you will be able to control your budget, bids and schedules.

Are you ready to create your own LinkedIn ads? Simply go to the "work" tab on your LinkedIn account dashboard and select "advertise", then click on the "create ad" button on the next page. From then on you will be able to select your ad type, customize your adverts and launch your campaign!

SMART WAYS TO GET LEADS ON LINKEDIN

Building a healthy pipeline of quality leads can be quite hard to achieve no matter where you are doing your marketing. But generating a good number of leads and referrals from any source doesn't have to be a daunting task, especially when you are doing it the right way.

That is why we have decided to show you the best ways to generate lots of leads to your business on LinkedIn, and we are going to do so in this video, where you will learn how to find, target and engage leads on the largest social platform for professionals.

Use the LinkedIn search function to identify qualifying leads

You don't generate leads by simply getting likes and comments, you get leads by connecting with the right audience. On LinkedIn, this means targeting the members the right way using the type of filters that will allow you to identify the best prospective individuals.

These filters include job titles, company roles, industry, and locations. Identifying the best prospects through these attributes will help you to only target those professionals that are more likely to understand the benefits offered by your product, service or business model.

Use LinkedIn to Connect with Qualifying Website Visitors

One of the greatest ways to tell when a lead can become a qualifying customer is when you can identify them through their browsing behavior. Specifically, you should be looking for people that visit your website as a sign of leads interested in your business.

Luckily, LinkedIn allows you to use a pixel code that you can add to your website, and you can use it to identify people that click through your website link from your profile or company page, which can help you to directly get in touch with these already qualifying leads. You can find this code and track your visitors from the "see who's viewed my profile" section.

Share Educational Content Through Your Profile

A really good way to capture people's attention and convert them into leads is by offering them a reason to do business with you through educational content. Now, there is a difference between sharing educational content through your profile and using lead magnets to capture people's contact info.

When you use a lead magnet you are basically offering a piece of free information that can be given in exchange for an email address or phone number, whereas sharing educational content is all about creating educational posts that offer value to people.

On LinkedIn, you can easily share educational content by using the "write an article" feature on the feed, and because this content is not going to be hidden behind an optin wall, anybody can access it. True qualifying leads will then flock to do business with you after seeing the value that your business has to offer!

Share Quality Advice on Groups

Groups can be an amazing source of leads if you know how to approach people that join. Just like on our previous point, a good way to qualify leads on groups is by offering them content with value and purpose, and in case of group members, this content has to be in the form of sound advice that responds to questions and needs posted by group members.

PREPARE A BUSINESS INTRO FOR YOUR PROFILES AND **Company Pages**

A business introduction for your profiles and company pages can't simply be a warm greeting. It has to be a fully-fledged explanation about what your company is, what it does and what it offers. Think of it as the mission statement of your website, only on your profiles and pages. Clear, concise business intros can help you to land leads without much effort.

HOW TO DO AFFILIATE MARKETING ON LINKEDIN

If you are among those that doesn't do affiliate marketing or, god forbid, still doesn't know what affiliate marketing is all about, please keep watching this video, because we are going to blow your mind with what we are about to show you.

Affiliate marketing, is marketing that is done to promote a product or service that you as a marketer don't stock on a retail level, but that you market to get a share of the profits made when the product sells through your own promotional efforts.

Affiliate marketing has become one of the favorite marketing methods of online marketers because it allows them to use their preferred outreach channels to offer prospective buyers stuff that is hard to resist.

And sometimes, just sometimes, affiliate marketing doesn't work for some people, and it is all because of their approach at promoting a product the wrong way, on the wrong channel. One such channel is social media, and in this chapter we are going to give you a leg up and help you to do affiliate marketing the right way on the LinkedIn platform!

Join Affiliate Marketing Groups

Using groups on LinkedIn is one of the best strategies if what you want is to achieve success with anything that you do on LinkedIn, and affiliate marketing is no exception! Groups are great for making information exchange easier, and this includes information that can help you to land some sweet affiliate deals.

Start by looking for affiliate marketing groups, which is easy to do, as you would only need to use affiliate related keywords or niche keywords. Affiliate marketing groups are a great source of knowledge because they're a home to experienced affiliate marketers, and affiliate posts don't look like spam in these groups.

Share Your LinkedIn Affiliate Offers on Other Social Channels

We have told you before how LinkedIn is different than other social channels, and the good thing about it is that you can use it to compliment your affiliate marketing efforts on other social media channels, especially on twitter.

Cross promoting your affiliate links on different social networking sites this way will help you to get more direct traffic to your offers.

Follow Company Pages Related to Your Niche

The most important thing that you can get as an affiliate

marketer are valid clicks to your offers and repeating customers, and the fact that only 3% of click throughs are likely to convert for any affiliate means that the traffic that you get to your offers has to be of the most relevant type possible.

And when you follow company pages that are related to your niche you increase your visibility to leads and prospective buyers that are also following them, increasing your chances of getting visits to your affiliate offers, and of getting sales through those offers as well.

Become a Content Expert

Being an affiliate marketer is not only about knowing how and where to post affiliate links, because if you want to become really successful at affiliate marketing you have to learn how to make people interested enough in your offers as to get them to click through them.

And there's no better way to do this than to become very knowledgeable about what you promote. Becoming an expert will allow you to create highly relevant content that can be the perfect placement for your affiliate links, and creating well informed affiliate articles and posts is the best way to get LinkedIn members to make informed purchases through your affiliate links!

Promote Free Info Products

Lead magnets can work wonders for affiliate marketing on LinkedIn when they offer valuable content for users, and you can spread your affiliate offers across the content offered inside your products.

Promote Your Affiliate Offers as Answers to Questions

Be on the lookout for questions made on the platform about products or services related to your offers, or questions made about problems that can be solved by using the products or services that you promote and subtly insert your affiliate links on your answers. Just remember to not write a sales pitch, but to suggest a solution.

USING THE LINKEDIN FEED FOR MARKET RESEARCH

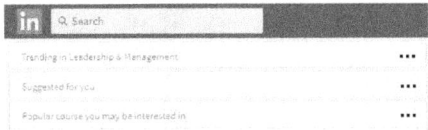

LINKEDIN IS NOT ONLY A PLATFORM TO DO MARKETING BUT also a place to find information about doing your marketing. Just like on any other social media platform, LinkedIn can give you access to a powerful depository of market information through its content discovery channels.

And just like on basically any other social networking site, this content discovery channel can be found right after you sign into your account, in the form of the updates feed. On LinkedIn, this feed follows a different approach because, while it might be used to share updates from the platform and its members, it does so only with serious, relevant content.

The basic functionality of this feed then is to show you what is trending and what is being shared both by your connections and content creators, and if you pay attention to the descriptions on top of each post you will find that a lot of these content pieces are being promoted on your feed in favor of other marketers that are targeting you as a potential lead, much like you would do as well.

The good news about this is that you can use all this information as market research data that you can later use for your own campaigns, which is as useful as it is practical because, as you can see, you can easily access all this information by simply scrolling down.

The first thing that you should note is that this feed will show you updates from pages and profiles that you follow. This information is important especially if you follow mostly companies in your niche, as the way in which LinkedIn members interact with this information will give you great insights into what is trending among your potential audience.

There are four specific types of content that will be continually featured on your LinkedIn feed. The first type of content is "recommended" content, which can be labeled as "trending", "recommended for you" or "popular".

These content pieces are curated both by LinkedIn's editorial team and by the platform's algorithm to serve only the most appropriate content to each member. The second type of content is content that is trending at the moment and that is labeled as "latest news" or as "mentioned in the news".

Unlike Recommended content, these posts are generally not curated or targeted towards any particular member based on its profile and its information, and they are only served for informational purposes, and they are also not intended to represent a given company's activities or point of view.

Now, "sponsored" content are content pieces that are intended to raise awareness about organizations, products, services or brands. In short, they are advertised material that is served either to members that follow a company page or that fit the criteria of an advertiser.

THESE CONTENT PIECES ARE NOT INTRUSIVE AND ARE DESIGNED to allow companies to build relationships and to generate quality leads by promoting content to people that would be difficult to reach otherwise.

As you can see, all the content that appears in your feed is relevant and customized according to your profile, and you can always manage the content that appears in your feed by hiding posts, by unfollowing companies that do not show you relevant content and by reporting content that might be inappropriate.

Remember that push notifications and emails are part of

the content on your feed, so make sure to leverage the information on your feed to see what's trending in the world of professional marketing on social media!

SMALL BUSINESS RESOURCES TO HELP YOU GET MORE OUT OF LINKEDIN

*E*verybody knows that, besides hard work and something great to offer, having the right type of relationships is the real key to business success, and LinkedIn has the right set of resources that can help any type of small business to get started.

After all, both small and normal sized businesses can use LinkedIn to build a brand that connects with the right type of people. A strong brand is what will help you to find and to be found by the best prospects.

The good news is that building a solid branding strategy that can attract more business opportunities on LinkedIn is as easy as creating a profile that can show others that you are an expert, which will get you noticed.

Then you will just have to expand your network and connect with business contacts that can help you to be more successful by creating new contacts and relationships that will take you further into your ventures. After achieving this, small businesses are invited to leverage the resources that LinkedIn has designed for them:

Branding

You can leverage LinkedIn's powerful platform to build a great reputation and increase your chances of driving new business relationships through branding.

Small business resources targeted at branding can help you to boost up your LinkedIn network, to win new clients through LinkedIn groups, to jump start new business ventures and to build business relationships that count both on LinkedIn as well as in the real world.

Marketing

No referrals are found without solid word of mouth, and referrals are what ultimately drive business, and LinkedIn can help you to generate buzz with awesome marketing solutions that are tailored for the small business of the digital age.

Marketing resources for small businesses include targeted ads on the LinkedIn platform that can easily help you to grow by directing your marketing efforts to the people that matter, and marketing on LinkedIn is a three step process that will start with you establishing your brand presence by creating a company page that can show your expertise and get your business noticed on the platform.

Then you will connect with your audience, which will help you to build a community of followers that is populated by the members of your target audience. And after you build your community, you will keep it engaged with valuable content.

Sales

You can use LinkedIn to find the right people whom to talk about your products and services. Finding the right leads and selling faster can be simplified by getting in touch with those that are more likely to want to close a deal with you.

Using LinkedIn with sales in mind is as easy as building a reputation that sells, finding the decision makers in any industry and getting them the information needed to close the deals. Tools such as the "sales navigator" and the educational resources provided by the LinkedIn platform will allow you to get way ahead of your competition when it comes to the sales department!

Hiring

Having the right type of hire in your team can make a big difference. It can even transform your business! And LinkedIn offers you the best recruiting tools for the job.

Building your employer brand, attracting the best candidates and then finding the best matches are the first steps. The second step is to use LinkedIn's hiring resources for small businesses such as job postings and the recruiter tools.

Get yourself ahead of the curve today and sign up for LinkedIn's awesome business resources!

GOING PREMIUM WITH LINKEDIN

LinkedIn is a great platform for business, no doubt about that. You can use it to maximize your chances of succeeding in your career or to find prospective clients, or to find funding for that awesome new business project of yours, one that you are sure will make headlines someday soon!

Everything that we just said is not praise that comes out of thin air because you already saw that you can achieve all of that stuff by simply creating a LinkedIn account and doing your homework. But can you improve on that? Yeah! You totally can by going premium, which you can do by clicking on the "Try Premium for free" link on your dashboard menu.

Now, when you go Premium you will be able to access LinkedIn features the same way that you would be able to on your normal, non-premium account, but with each one of them turned up to eleven and on turbo mode.

As you can see here, you can select a different plan depending on what's your goal. The "Career" plan, for example, will allow you to get hired and get ahead by getting in touch with hiring managers, to see how you compare to other members and learn new skills to advance in your career. This plan is mostly for people looking to grow professionally on the platform.

But we have established by now that your goal is to grow your business, and there is also a set of plans to help you along the way with that specifically. The "Business" plan for instance is designed to help you grow and nurture your network by finding the right people, promoting your business and learning new skills to enhance your business brand.

You can select a premium plan on a free trial for a period of a month, and in the case of the "business" plan it's going to be $47.99 a month after your free trial period expires. Features included with your "business" premium plan include 15 InMail messages, business insights, online video courses, the ability to see who has viewed your profile, unlimited profile browsing and career insights.

The "Sales" plan, on the other hand, is designed to help you unlock sales opportunities finding leads and accounts in your target market, getting real time insights for warm outreach and to build closer business relationships based on trust with customers and prospects.

It is $64.99 a month after your free trial and its features include 20 InMail messages, sales insights, advanced search with the "lead builder" tool, and lead recommendations as well as saved leads, alongside the features offered by the "Business plan".

Lastly, the "Hiring" plan is designed to help you find and hire talent and great job candidates for your organization faster. With this plan you will be able to contact top talent directly and build great relationships with prospective hires.

The "Hiring" plan is $99.50 a month after the trial expires and includes features such as 30 InMail messages, advanced search functions, smart suggestions, integrated hiring, automatic candidate tracking and recruiting specific design, alongside the features offered by the "Sales" plan.

Once you have decided which Premium plan best suits your needs simply click on the "start my free month" and try it out!

DO'S AND DON'TS

As with any business venture that you decide to partake in, LinkedIn marketing and doing business on LinkedIn has its recommended practices and its things to avoid. Most marketers have to learn all of them the hard way through trial and error, but we have created this video so you can get it right from the get go!

Do's

Do keep your profiles and company pages professional. Remember that both are crucial because they are designed to foster a community around your business, your products, and your services, and they're also the very first thing that people will find when they are looking for your brand.

Do optimize your company pages for search engines. The company pages not only have to be tidy and professional looking, they also have to be functional, so remember to use your targeted keywords in the "about" section of your page, as this section is indexed by search engines.

Do participate on LinkedIn groups and discussions. This will not only help you to engage with your audience, but it will also help you to learn what is being said about your brand, your niche, your products, services, and about your competition.

Do make use of rich media to share your content. Professionals not only love it when relevant content is served through videos, presentations and well-crafted articles, it also helps them to perceive the messenger as an authority in the subject matter, so make sure to create relevant content that is well presented.

Do vary the type of content that you share with your business audience. People can easily gravitate towards other companies if you only talk about your business, so consider sharing other types of relevant content such as industry news and links to other pages.

Do keep your business invitation well thought out and professional. Nothing puts a prospective connection off like a dry invitational message. Forget about using the template invitation and instead take your time and personalize the invitations that you send to professionals that you look forward to making your connections with on the platform.

Do cross promote through your LinkedIn profiles and company pages. There is a reason why the "about" section is in there, so you can easily share your up to date company links with the people that are most likely to click there.

Do follow any other company in your industry with a LinkedIn profile or page. Remember that, on LinkedIn, these other pages are not necessarily your competition, but potential prospects as well. Keeping up to date with other companies is a great way to know whom to collaborate with when the time comes.

Do request other companies to link up with their current employees. This will not only increase your brand visibility, but it will also allow you to increase your business connections, which will in turn increase your opportunities of keeping up with future talent prospects!

Do stay connected on a much more personal level by using the "relationships tab", which will allow you to set up personalized communications with your prospects. Remember that people are prone to become company champions when they receive personalized communication with a brand, which means that they will market your brand to others!

Don'ts

Don't focus your LinkedIn marketing efforts on selling, ever. LinkedIn is a platform where people go to establish professional connections, and any sales approach will immediately put them off. If you want to sell on LinkedIn, focus on offering value first!

Don't join just any LinkedIn group just because you can. Doing this will not only detract your time and effort from where they should be focused on, it will also make your company look like a scam. Focus instead only on groups that are specific to your industry.

Don't forget to be proactive. What happens after you join a group on LinkedIn? You become an authority, that's what. But you have to put in the effort by participating constantly, in a natural way. This will do wonders for your marketing efforts because people will gravitate to your brand thanks to its vocal, interactive nature.

Don't forget about the human factor. A lot of companies fail miserably at communication because they forget to give a human touch to their online presence. Your interactions, your posts, your responses and your participation have to feel like a real human is doing it, so remember to be natural and friendly!

Don't be too complex. Many businesses confuse being smart with being complicated, and they end up populating their marketing materials with long, overtly scripted, and full of company jargon copy. Instead, focus on being concise and to the point. People will appreciate it!

Don't forget about tracking your marketing performance. There is data out there that will easily tell you when you are doing well and when you need to improve. Stuff such as leads generated, successful connections and strategic partnerships are great indicators of efficient LinkedIn marketing efforts!

Don't spam on LinkedIn. Now, you might be used to the casual promotional sales message on other social networks, but even the smallest hint of a sale is considered spam on LinkedIn. Remember that here you need to communicate that you care about people more than your product, not the other way around!

Don't let your profiles and company pages sit still. Groups are not the only way to stay active, as profiles and company pages are excellent marketing tools as long as you only use them to give relevant advice that can lead to a sale later on.

Don't use LinkedIn to criticize other products or competing companies. Doing so simply looks unprofessional. On the other hand, mentioning bigger companies in a positive light can direct quality traffic from their pages to yours!

Don't forget about nurturing your communications by always checking and replying to messages and comments left by LinkedIn members on your company pages. This seemingly simple action can be more effective than paid advertising in some instances!

PREMIUM TOOLS AND SERVICES TO CONSIDER

LinkedIn in itself can be considered one of the most powerful marketing tools available in recent memory because it allows you to smoothly run your promotional campaigns on the very first social network targeted at professionals, which can immensely widen the reach of your business by the very nature of the audience that you'll be able to serve content to on the platform.

But because LinkedIn is so good at allowing you to do that one single thing, to market to a professional audience, you would greatly benefit from integrating third party functionality to your LinkedIn marketing. The following is a list of premium tools and services that can help you to up the ante!

LinkedIn Dominator

The LinkedInDominator is a one of a kind automation tool for LinkedIn marketers, a tool that will allow you to easily build marketing lists with a very powerful and intuitive piece of software. In other words, it will allow you to reach the over 300 million registered users in the platform if that is your aim, the easy way.

LinkedInDominator is an efficient tool that you can use to manage and automate your LinkedIn marketing campaigns and efforts. For example, it can help you to gather data that can be essential to your social marketing campaigns on the LinkedIn platform. LinkedInDominator does this by simply scraping data from search URLs and with the use of filters.

LinkedInDominator can also add connections to your account on autopilot to increase your marketing success. It can easily send automated invitations either through email or through keyword searches.

LinkedInDominator can also help you to manage multiple accounts the right way by loading multiple accounts from within a single URL and by deleting or swapping inactive or irrelevant accounts from your inventory.

Also, as you might know, groups are vital to your marketing plans, and on account of this LinkedInDominator can automate your group status updates, to use filters to track and invite new members to your groups and to remove unwanted group members.

Crystal

One of the main goals of a LinkedIn marketing campaign is to also find out who your potential prospects and customers will be by refining who you target with your campaigns by continually educating yourself with the help of the large amount of data that each marketing campaign trail brings to your table.

Yet assessing how your prospects qualify by looking at the profile data can be an excruciating task after the fact, and it is seriously some expert level stuff that you will have to deal with, which will give you different results than you expected in the long run.

That is why it would be amazing to have a tool that could give you an exact reading of your prospects, and "crystal" has been designed to give you exactly that: it reviews the information provided on any given LinkedIn page or profile to help you assess a prospect's personality.

And you can use this information to increase your chances of effectively communicating with that prospect or organization, on their own terms. This means that the approach works for satisfying your prospect's needs as well as your marketing goals.

"Crystal" will allow you to achieve this by importing your contacts from LinkedIn and giving you a personality report based on the information gathered from their personal or corporate profiles. Crystal is so effective at this, in fact, that it can give you real time advice on how to craft personalized emails and invitations while you compose them!

"Crystal" can also analyze text from social media, which means that it will analyze the content of your interactions with others on LinkedIn groups and on comments left on your company pages.

LeadFuze

One of the greatest strengths of the LinkedIn platform can easily become your greatest weakness; namely, the amount of data that you have to examine and sort through can be overwhelming once you realize that you will be dealing with more than 300 million registered users.

And as any marketer or business with even the slightest idea of what it takes to run a successful marketing campaign that drives real results, getting leads is the hardest part of the equation when you have a giant target audience in front of you.

LeadFuze has been designed to make lead generation easy and automated. LeadFuze is all about marketing consistency, and that is why it offers LinkedIn users a software based platform that does all the grunt work for them.

It can automate lead generating efforts by finding your prospects with the use of data filters that include job title, location and industry. LeadFuze is so effective that it automatically pulls up information such as email addresses, phone numbers, company, domain name of their website, and social media profiles.

It then automates your personalized outreach by sending a series of emails to your prospects, then sending a series of follow ups if they don't respond in a designated amount of time. It gives you a full report of your automated marketing and outreach efforts, and it seamlessly integrates with additional contact, support and marketing platforms.

SalesTool

Now, if what you need is a simpler way to collect your data because of technical or time constraints, or just because you believe that less is more, Salestool is the perfect solution for you because it will allow you to import lists of leads from LinkedIn right to your computer in Excel format.

And that is not the only thing that is made easier with Salestool, because it can also simplify live data search by allowing you to gather information from any website such as LinkedIn in three simple steps: press the plugin icon on your browser, look at the data stack and then save your list of prospects to your computer or online platform database with a few clicks.

The best part is that the information is kept up to date in real time, storing prospective information such as seniority or department.

SHOCKING CASE STUDIES

The following are the stories of some of the businesses and marketers that have successfully used LinkedIn as a platform to launch their online campaigns and have reached their goals in the process, even surpassing their initial expectations by a long shot. Use them as inspiration to keep growing!

Aspect

Aspect is a company specialized in customer satisfaction software. Their primary product is the delivery of great software based solutions that help companies of all sizes to deliver seamless, uncompromising customer experiences across any conversation and channel.

The company stated that their main objective was to promote thought leadership oriented content to decision makers in the IT and customer experience industries. They also wanted to attract more qualifying traffic to their company website and blog.

The Company made use of LinkedIn's marketing platform to perform their duties by using Promoted Content advertising to promote white papers, webinars and infographics. They mainly targeted job titles, from IT managers and above.

The results were amazing to say the least, with an increase of over 322% in engagement on LinkedIn, a 290% increase in traffic to the company's website and blog, and a 17% increase in the number of followers on their company page!

Bynder

Bynder is a software company focused on delivery only the highest quality when it comes to digital asset management, branding automation and marketing solutions. It offers companies the right tools to easily create, find and use the right type of content.

When Bynder launched their award winning digital asset management platform in 2013, they faced the challenge of having to compete with entities that were established, so their objective was to generate a healthy amount of sales leads amongst enterprise-level prospects.

The Company used LinkedIn to deliver original content that could be used as digital assets that were tailored for different stages of the buyer journey, such as their "Digital Assets Management for Dummies" guide, sponsored content that was personalized for different sized businesses and by using LinkedIn lead generating forms pre-filled with profile data pulled from the platform.

Bynder beat all its cost per acquisition targets by delivering a conversion rate to leads that was close to 2%, which was achieved in the first five months of the campaign. Also, the completion rate of lead generation forms jumped to 20%, and the rate at which leads were generated skyrocketed to 500%!

BlackRock

BlackRock is currently the largest asset manager for individuals, companies, financial professionals and institutions in the world. It has a large portfolio of clients from all around the globe and from all walks of life, and its mission is as simple as it is noble: to help people and companies of all sizes to achieve a better financial future.

BlackRock's objective was to deepen the understanding that potential clients had about its brand, and to achieve this objective the Company decided to target and engage sophisticated investors with highly relevant content.

The Company used LinkedIn as a platform for content distribution and user engagement by streamlining communication and engagement with its target audience through sponsored content posts. This strategy allowed BlackRock to reach qualifying clients with basic educational information as well as with detailed asset management material.

BlackRock was able to truly reach a uniquely targeted and niche audience through its partnership with LinkedIn, acquiring over 222,000 followers on its company page, breaking industry benchmarks for engagement rates by four times, outperforming its competitors, and increasing its brand value by 2%.

Callaway Golf

Callaway Golf is an American sports company that designs, manufactures, markets and sells golf related products such as equipment and accessories, as well as life style products centered on the game of golf, and distributes them to more than 70 countries.

The objective of the company was to broaden its reach by reenergizing its brand through a marketing campaign geared towards its more digitally inclined prospects, which incidentally are digitally connected professionals with a shared passion for golf.

LinkedIn is home to Callaway Golf's perfect target audience, which is comprised by a demographic of professional individuals who are also golf lovers. They used the LinkedIn platform to launch an app called "Hit the Links", which allowed the company to collect information from member profiles through the LinkedIn API.

The Company's strategy worked like a charm and proved that brands have a large impact when market players can see its audience not only engaging with an interactive campaign launched by the brand's parent company, but also encouraging other people to engage as well.

The company gained 1,500 new followers on its company page, an 83% lift in positive sentiment towards the company on the social platform and a 32% increase in open rates for its sponsored email content.

ConnectWise

ConnectWise is one of the world's leading companies in the world of business management systems. With over 100,000 users worldwide, ConnectWise allows individuals and companies to integrate business process automations such as help desk, customer service, sales, marketing, project management and analytics under one roof.

The Company needed to increase the number of leads delivered to its sales team, and they decided to use LinkedIn because they knew that it was the perfect marketing channel thanks to its powerful targeting features.

They also wanted to generate better insight reports on how their marketing campaigns were performing on LinkedIn as well as on other platforms.

The solution to their requirements was to use conversion tracking with sponsored content to track campaign effectiveness as well as return on investment, and they did so by simply checking in their LinkedIn Campaign Manager. They only had to integrate the LinkedIn Insight Tag on their site and they were ready to get it rolling out.

Since then ConnectWise has been getting nothing short of spectacular and ongoing results, including conversion rates that double the average conversion rates on LinkedIn by a cool 2% thanks to sponsored content campaigns.

FREQUENTLY ASKED QUESTIONS

So now you have completed the whole circle and have learned how to operate the LinkedIn for Business platform on your own, but it might happen that you will find yourself in need of a helping hand along the way on things that may only surface while you grow in the platform.

Thinking about that, we have designed a frequently asked questions video with a curated list of questions that are frequently asked even by advanced "LinkedIn for Business" users, so let's take a look at some of the things that you can be prepared to solve the easy way some time in the future.

Is it a good idea to include contact information in the "Name" or in the headline information fields on LinkedIn? Will that increase your chances at getting more connections?

You can do that because it isn't something that goes

against LinkedIn's terms of service, but you shouldn't do it because, on one hand, it looks pretty unprofessional. In fact, doing that will make your profiles and company pages look like outright scams.

On the other hand, it reduces the space that you should be dedicating to keywords that can actually help your business to be found, and that can also help your pages to improve their search engine rankings.

Is it a good practice to include your contact information even when you have a company page for your business already populated with information about your business?

Yes, your contact information should be part of your profile. Remember that you are on LinkedIn to widen your business' reach, and your contact information is a great way to organically market yourself as a representative of your business.

Of course, this contact information should be through your own business to further increase the effectiveness of your marketing efforts. To give you an example, the email address in your profile should be under the domain name of your business website and not under a generic email provider such as Gmail. Another example is your phone number, which should be your work phone and not your personal phone number.

Including this information in your profile also increases your business' visibility on search engines because it is indexed from your LinkedIn profile, from your Company pages and from your company website. This is organic marketing in its purest form!

How often should you update your business profiles and company pages?

While there is not a single outline of how often you should update your profiles and pages on LinkedIn, the best practice is to update them as regularly as needed. This is because constant activity helps your profiles and pages to be perceived as being in line with market trends.

Can you backup your profiles and pages?

Yes, you can backup your profiles and pages by going to the three-dotted button on the top of the screen so you can save a copy of your profile or page in PDF format.

Is there a way to track the performance of your business marketing efforts on LinkedIn that can give you the whole picture?

There is actually a way to easily track how well you are performing as a business marketer on the LinkedIn platform by keeping a 90-day record of the following information during that time frame:

- Number of connections made
- The number of profile or page views
- How many times your business appears in search results
- The number of emails and sponsored emails
- How many business opportunities have surfaced

- How many updates and content posts you have shared

What happens if there is already a company page for your business on LinkedIn?

It can happen that someone has already created a page for your company right before you create it. This mostly happens when people working for your organization or that are part of your organization in some way create a company page to be added to their profiles to showcase their work experience or the place where they are currently working.

In such cases, you can easily claim ownership of the company page by clicking the three dotted button on the top of the company page and clicking on "claim this page" from the dropdown menu.

Just remember that before claiming ownership of a page you need to add and confirm the email address that you use at your company and to list your current position within the company in your profile.

What are the steps to become successful at marketing on LinkedIn?

As anything else in life, marketing your business on LinkedIn is no magic bullet, but the simple act of creating a profile and a company page on the platform is a great start. Of course, there are some things that you can do in order to achieve greater success as a LinkedIn marketer:

First you have to create powerful profiles and company pages that complement each other. Your profile and the company page for your business should be set up as different organs of the same entity, because information about your business on both placements is great for driving organic outreach.

Secondly, you have to build a network. Do not wait to get followers just because you joined an industry group, you need to be proactive in reaching out to the people that are most likely to connect with your brand.

A great way to establish authority as a marketer and as a brand on LinkedIn is by constantly responding to queries made by people in your industry in the questions and answers section.

So how does LinkedIn work for businesses if they want to drive sales when LinkedIn is better suited for people looking for jobs and recruiters?

It works because marketing a business, a product or a service on LinkedIn is a great way to drive sales of customers that are in a different league, such as managers, distributors and investors from overseas.

We hope that you can use this information to get lots of business opportunities as well as qualifying leads and useful insights!

www.ingramcontent.com/pod-product-compliance
Lightning Source LLC
Chambersburg PA
CBHW070307230526
45470CB00002B/756